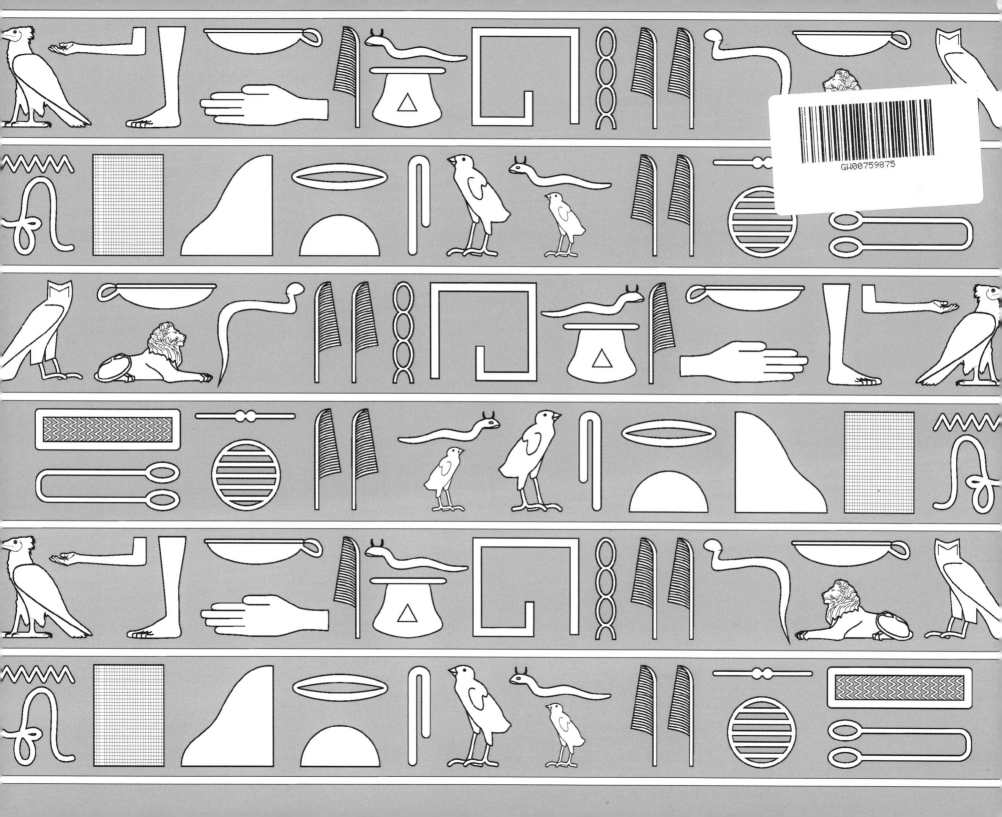

Kheru Nefer: Beautiful Night Kings and Queens

Written by Obi Shaaim Maa

Illustrated by Metu DeggKhet

Kheru Nefer: Beautiful Night (Kings and Queens) 0-6

A children's history book about ancient Egypt (Kemet).

Published by:

Our Communities Our Children Publishing LLC

1205 Atlantic Avenue, Suite 472585

Brooklyn, N.Y. 11216

Website: www.OCOCbooks.com

Author: Obi Shaaim Maa

Illustrations: Metu DeggKhet

Cover: Metu DeggKhet

Graphics: Metu DeggKhet

ISBN: 978-1-953952-06-6

Library of Congress Control Number: 2021946728

Our Communities Our Children ®

Dedicated to the ancestors of Ancient Kemet (Egypt).

Table of Contents

Kheru Nefer: Beautiful Night
(Kings and Queens) Ages 0 to 6

Narmer and Neithhotep
3150 – 2613 BCE

This king and queen made people come together. That is how they tried to make Egypt live forever.

Djoser and Hetephernebti
2686-2648 BCE

This king and queen, the first pyramid they did make. It stands in Egypt to this date.

Khufu and Henutsen
2589-2566 BCE

This king and queen, the biggest pyramid they did create. That is why we call that pyramid "**The Great**".

Mentuhotep II and Neferu II
2055-2004 BCE

This king and queen made bad people go away. They made Egypt a safe place to stay.

Senusret I and Neferu III
1965-1920 BCE

This king and queen made their country grow. Egypt became a place that all people would know.

Senusret III and Neferthenut
1878 to 1839 BCE

This king and queen made art and culture flow. They made Egypt rich and made it glow.

Ahmose and Ahmose-Nefertari
1550-1525 BCE

This king and queen took land to make Egypt big and fine. They built temples and tombs that stand through time.

Thutmose I and Queen Ahmose
1504-1492 BCE

This king and queen made Egypt grow large. Their army told others who was in charge.

Queen Hatshepsut and Thutmose II
1479-1425 BCE

This king and queen made large temples all over Egypt. They are still there, so you can believe it.

Thutmose III and Merytre-Hatshepsut
1479-1425 BCE

This king and queen kept their country the strongest. This allowed Egypt to last the longest.

Amenhotep III and Tiye
1390-1353 BCE

This king and queen helped people grow food and build homes. They made Egypt the richest country ever known.

Glossary

Kheru Nefer: Beautiful Night

(Kings and Queens) Glossary (Ages 0 to 6)

Ancient Egypt: A seven thousand year old country in east Africa.

Army: A group of men and women who fight for a country.

Build: To make something.

Country: Land that people make their own.

Create: To make something.

Culture: A way of living.

Great: Big or important.

Grow: To make big or become big.

Large: Big.

King: Male or man ruler of a nation, people or group.

Pyramid: A big three-sided building used as a tomb.

Queen: Female or woman ruler of a nation, people or group.

Rich/Richest: To have all the things you need.

Ruler: One who serves and controls a nation, people or group.

Temple: A place where people pray.

Tomb: A place for the dead.

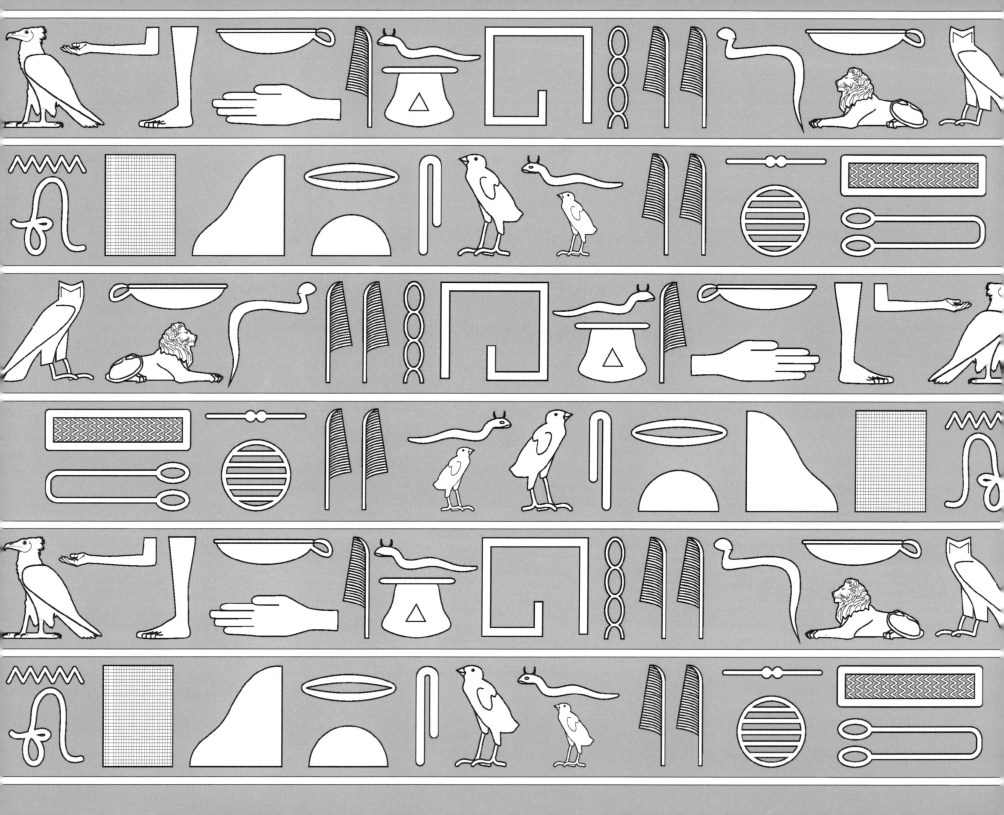

Lightning Source UK Ltd.
Milton Keynes UK
UKRC031408151021
392261UK00001B/7